55 Low Carbohydrate Recipes for Home

By: Kelly Johnson

Table of Contents

Breakfast:

- Avocado and Bacon Egg Cups
- Spinach and Feta Omelette
- Keto Chia Seed Pudding
- Zucchini and Cheese Muffins
- Smoked Salmon and Cream Cheese Roll-Ups

Lunch:

- Grilled Chicken Caesar Salad Lettuce Wraps
- Broccoli and Cheddar Soup
- Turkey and Avocado Lettuce Wraps
- Cauliflower Fried Rice
- Caprese Salad Skewers

Dinner:

- Baked Lemon Garlic Butter Salmon
- Spaghetti Squash with Pesto and Cherry Tomatoes
- Cauliflower Crust Pizza
- Shrimp Stir-Fry with Vegetables
- Eggplant Lasagna

Snacks:

- Guacamole with Veggie Sticks
- Parmesan Crisps
- Deviled Eggs
- Buffalo Cauliflower Bites
- Cucumber and Cream Cheese Bites

Sides:

- Roasted Brussels Sprouts with Bacon
- Garlic Butter Asparagus
- Creamy Cauliflower Mash

- Sauteed Green Beans with Almonds
- Jicama Fries with Chipotle Mayo

Desserts:

- Keto Chocolate Avocado Pudding
- Almond Flour Chocolate Chip Cookies
- Berry Coconut Chia Seed Popsicles
- Lemon Cheesecake Fat Bombs
- Dark Chocolate Dipped Strawberries

Smoothies:

- Green Keto Smoothie with Avocado and Spinach
- Berry and Broccoli Stir-Fry
- Cabbage and Ground Turkey Skillet
- Salmon and Avocado Salad
- Eggplant and Zucchini Gratin

Soups:

- Tomato Basil Soup with Heavy Cream
- Cabbage and Sausage Soup
- Creamy Broccoli and Cheese Soup
- Chicken Zoodle Soup
- Spinach and Artichoke Soup

Salads:

- Cobb Salad with Ranch Dressing
- Greek Salad with Feta and Olives
- Avocado and Shrimp Salad
- Kale and Walnut Salad with Lemon Vinaigrette
- Tuna Salad Lettuce Wraps

Dips:

- Baba Ganoush
- Spinach and Artichoke Dip
- Cilantro Lime Avocado Dip
- Pimento Cheese Dip

- Roasted Red Pepper Hummus

Breakfast:

Avocado and Bacon Egg Cups

Ingredients:

- 2 ripe avocados
- 4 large eggs
- 4 slices of bacon
- Salt and pepper, to taste
- Chopped chives or parsley for garnish (optional)

Instructions:

Preheat the Oven:

    Preheat your oven to 375°F (190°C).
    Prepare Avocados:
- Cut the avocados in half, and remove the pits.
- Using a spoon, scoop out a small portion of the flesh from each avocado half to make room for the egg.

Wrap with Bacon:
- Carefully wrap each avocado half with a slice of bacon, making sure the bacon is secured around the edges.

Place in Baking Dish:
- Place the bacon-wrapped avocado halves in a baking dish or on a baking sheet.

Crack Eggs:
- Crack an egg into each avocado half, ensuring the yolk stays intact.

Season:
- Sprinkle salt and pepper over each egg according to your taste.

Bake:
- Bake in the preheated oven for about 15-20 minutes or until the eggs reach your desired level of doneness. The bacon should be crispy.

Garnish:
- If desired, garnish with chopped chives or parsley.

Serve:
- Carefully remove from the oven and serve immediately.

This recipe is not only delicious but also provides a balance of creamy avocado, savory bacon, and the richness of a perfectly baked egg. Adjust the baking time based on your preference for the egg's doneness. Enjoy your Avocado and Bacon Egg Cups!

Spinach and Feta Omelette

Ingredients:

- 3 large eggs
- 1/2 cup fresh spinach, chopped
- 1/4 cup feta cheese, crumbled
- 2 tablespoons milk (optional, for a fluffier omelette)
- Salt and pepper, to taste
- 1 tablespoon olive oil or butter for cooking
- Fresh herbs (such as parsley) for garnish (optional)

Instructions:

Prepare Ingredients:
- Chop the fresh spinach and crumble the feta cheese.

Whisk Eggs:
- Crack the eggs into a bowl and whisk them together until well combined. If you prefer a fluffier omelette, you can add milk to the beaten eggs and whisk again.

Season Eggs:
- Season the beaten eggs with salt and pepper according to your taste.

Preheat Pan:
- Heat olive oil or butter in a non-stick skillet over medium heat.

Cook Spinach:
- Add the chopped spinach to the skillet and sauté for about 1-2 minutes until wilted.

Pour in Eggs:
- Pour the beaten eggs over the spinach in the skillet.

Add Feta:
- Sprinkle crumbled feta cheese evenly over one half of the omelette.

Cooking the Omelette:
- Allow the eggs to set around the edges. With a spatula, gently lift the edges to let the uncooked eggs flow underneath.

Fold and Serve:
- Once the eggs are mostly set but still slightly runny on top, fold the omelette in half using the spatula.

Final Touch:
- Cook for an additional 1-2 minutes until the omelette is cooked through but still moist inside.

Garnish and Serve:
- Slide the omelette onto a plate, garnish with fresh herbs if desired, and serve immediately.

This Spinach and Feta Omelette is a nutritious and flavorful breakfast option. Feel free to customize it with additional ingredients such as tomatoes, onions, or mushrooms based on your preferences. Enjoy!

Keto Chia Seed Pudding

Ingredients:

- 1/4 cup chia seeds
- 1 cup unsweetened almond milk or coconut milk
- 1-2 tablespoons of your preferred low-carb sweetener (like stevia or erythritol)
- 1/2 teaspoon vanilla extract
- Optional toppings: sliced strawberries, raspberries, or a dollop of whipped cream (ensure they fit your keto requirements)

Instructions:

Mix Ingredients:
- In a bowl, combine chia seeds, almond milk (or coconut milk), sweetener, and vanilla extract.

Stir Well:
- Stir the mixture well to ensure that the chia seeds are evenly distributed.

Refrigerate:
- Cover the bowl and refrigerate the mixture for at least 2 hours, or overnight. This allows the chia seeds to absorb the liquid and create a pudding-like consistency.

Stir Again:
- After the initial refrigeration period, give the mixture another good stir. If it seems too thick, you can add a bit more almond milk to achieve your desired consistency.

Refrigerate Again:
- Place the mixture back in the refrigerator for an additional 1-2 hours or until it reaches the thickness you prefer.

Serve:
- Once the chia pudding has reached the desired consistency, serve it in individual bowls or jars.

Add Toppings:
- Top the chia seed pudding with your favorite keto-friendly toppings, such as sliced berries or a dollop of whipped cream.

Enjoy:
- Enjoy your keto chia seed pudding as a delicious and satisfying low-carb dessert or breakfast!

This keto chia seed pudding is not only easy to make but also a versatile dish that you can customize to suit your taste. Adjust the sweetness and toppings based on your preferences while keeping it within your keto dietary restrictions.

Zucchini and Cheese Muffins

Ingredients:

- 2 cups grated zucchini (about 2 medium-sized zucchinis)
- 1 1/2 cups shredded cheddar cheese
- 2 cups almond flour
- 1/4 cup coconut flour
- 1 teaspoon baking powder
- 1/2 teaspoon baking soda
- 1/2 teaspoon salt
- 1/2 teaspoon garlic powder
- 1/4 teaspoon black pepper
- 4 large eggs
- 1/4 cup melted butter or coconut oil
- 1/4 cup sour cream or Greek yogurt

Instructions:

Preheat Oven:
- Preheat your oven to 350°F (175°C). Line a muffin tin with paper liners or grease it well.

Prepare Zucchini:
- Grate the zucchinis using a box grater. Squeeze out excess moisture from the grated zucchini using a clean kitchen towel or paper towels.

Combine Dry Ingredients:
- In a large bowl, whisk together almond flour, coconut flour, baking powder, baking soda, salt, garlic powder, and black pepper.

Combine Wet Ingredients:
- In a separate bowl, beat the eggs. Add melted butter or coconut oil and sour cream (or Greek yogurt). Mix well.

Mix Wet and Dry Ingredients:
- Add the wet ingredients to the dry ingredients and stir until just combined.

Add Zucchini and Cheese:
- Fold in the grated zucchini and shredded cheddar cheese into the batter.

Fill Muffin Cups:
- Spoon the batter into the muffin cups, filling each about two-thirds full.

Bake:
- Bake in the preheated oven for 20-25 minutes or until the muffins are golden brown and a toothpick inserted into the center comes out clean.

Cool:
- Allow the muffins to cool in the tin for a few minutes before transferring them to a wire rack to cool completely.

Serve:
- Enjoy the zucchini and cheese muffins warm or at room temperature.

These muffins are a great way to incorporate zucchini into your diet while enjoying a tasty and savory snack. Feel free to customize the recipe by adding herbs or spices to suit your taste preferences.

Smoked Salmon and Cream Cheese Roll-Ups

Ingredients:

- 8 slices of smoked salmon
- 8 oz (about 225g) cream cheese, softened
- 1 tablespoon fresh dill, chopped
- 1 tablespoon capers, drained (optional)
- 1 tablespoon red onion, finely chopped
- Zest of 1 lemon
- Black pepper, to taste
- Lemon wedges, for serving
- Fresh chives or additional dill for garnish (optional)

Instructions:

Prepare Cream Cheese Mixture:
- In a bowl, combine the softened cream cheese, chopped dill, capers (if using), chopped red onion, lemon zest, and black pepper. Mix well until all ingredients are evenly incorporated.

Assemble Roll-Ups:
- Lay out the smoked salmon slices on a clean surface. Spread a thin layer of the cream cheese mixture evenly over each slice of smoked salmon.

Roll the Salmon:
- Starting from one end, carefully roll up each slice of smoked salmon with the cream cheese filling. Repeat for all slices.

Chill:
- Place the rolled-up smoked salmon and cream cheese in the refrigerator for at least 30 minutes to allow them to firm up.

Slice and Garnish:
- Once chilled, use a sharp knife to slice the rolls into bite-sized pieces, about 1-inch thick.

Garnish:
- Garnish with additional dill or fresh chives if desired.

Serve:
- Arrange the smoked salmon and cream cheese roll-ups on a serving platter. Serve with lemon wedges on the side.

Enjoy:
- Enjoy these delightful smoked salmon and cream cheese roll-ups as an appetizer or snack.

These roll-ups are not only delicious but also elegant, making them a perfect addition to a brunch or party spread. Feel free to customize by adding ingredients like cucumber slices or avocado for extra flavor and texture.

Lunch:

Grilled Chicken Caesar Salad Lettuce Wraps

Ingredients:

For the Grilled Chicken:

- 2 boneless, skinless chicken breasts
- 1 tablespoon olive oil
- Salt and pepper to taste
- 1 teaspoon garlic powder
- 1 teaspoon dried oregano
- 1 teaspoon paprika

For the Caesar Dressing:

- 1/2 cup mayonnaise
- 1/4 cup grated Parmesan cheese
- 2 tablespoons lemon juice
- 1 tablespoon Dijon mustard
- 2 cloves garlic, minced
- Salt and pepper to taste

For the Salad:

- Romaine lettuce leaves, washed and dried
- Cherry tomatoes, halved
- Croutons
- Shaved Parmesan cheese

Instructions:

Preheat the grill to medium-high heat.
In a small bowl, mix together the olive oil, salt, pepper, garlic powder, oregano, and paprika to create a marinade for the chicken.
Place the chicken breasts in a resealable plastic bag and pour the marinade over them. Seal the bag and massage the marinade into the chicken. Allow it to marinate for at least 15-30 minutes.

Grill the chicken breasts for about 6-8 minutes per side or until they are cooked through and have nice grill marks. Make sure the internal temperature reaches 165°F (74°C). Remove from the grill and let them rest for a few minutes before slicing.

While the chicken is grilling, prepare the Caesar dressing by whisking together mayonnaise, Parmesan cheese, lemon juice, Dijon mustard, minced garlic, salt, and pepper in a bowl. Adjust the seasoning to taste.

Once the chicken has rested, slice it into thin strips.

To assemble the lettuce wraps, take a romaine lettuce leaf and spoon a bit of the Caesar dressing onto it. Add a few slices of grilled chicken, cherry tomatoes, croutons, and shaved Parmesan cheese.

Repeat the process for the remaining lettuce wraps.

Serve immediately and enjoy your Grilled Chicken Caesar Salad Lettuce Wraps! You can customize the toppings and dressing according to your preferences.

Broccoli and Cheddar Soup

Ingredients:

- 4 cups fresh broccoli florets, chopped
- 1 small onion, finely chopped
- 2 carrots, peeled and diced
- 2 cloves garlic, minced
- 1/4 cup unsalted butter
- 1/4 cup all-purpose flour
- 3 cups chicken or vegetable broth
- 2 cups milk
- 2 cups shredded sharp cheddar cheese
- Salt and pepper, to taste
- 1/4 teaspoon nutmeg (optional)
- 1/2 cup heavy cream (optional, for added creaminess)

Instructions:

In a large pot, melt the butter over medium heat. Add the chopped onion and cook until it becomes translucent, about 3-5 minutes.
Stir in the minced garlic and cook for an additional 1-2 minutes until fragrant.
Sprinkle the flour over the onion and garlic mixture, stirring continuously to create a roux. Cook for 2-3 minutes to remove the raw flour taste.
Slowly whisk in the chicken or vegetable broth, ensuring there are no lumps. Add the milk gradually, continuing to whisk until well combined.
Add the chopped broccoli and diced carrots to the pot. Bring the mixture to a simmer and cook for about 15-20 minutes or until the vegetables are tender.
Using an immersion blender, blend the soup until it reaches your desired consistency. Alternatively, transfer a portion of the soup to a blender and blend in batches, being careful not to overfill the blender.
Return the blended soup to the pot over low heat. Stir in the shredded cheddar cheese until melted and smooth.
Season the soup with salt, pepper, and nutmeg (if using). If you prefer a creamier texture, stir in the heavy cream.
Allow the soup to simmer for an additional 5-10 minutes to let the flavors meld.
Taste and adjust the seasonings if necessary. Serve hot, garnished with additional shredded cheddar cheese if desired.

Enjoy your homemade Broccoli and Cheddar Soup! It pairs well with crusty bread or crackers for a satisfying meal.

Turkey and Avocado Lettuce Wraps

Ingredients:

- 1 lb ground turkey
- 1 tablespoon olive oil
- 1 teaspoon ground cumin
- 1 teaspoon chili powder
- 1/2 teaspoon garlic powder
- 1/2 teaspoon onion powder
- Salt and pepper, to taste
- 1 large avocado, sliced
- 1 cup cherry tomatoes, halved
- 1/2 red onion, finely diced
- Juice of 1 lime
- Fresh cilantro, chopped (optional)
- Iceberg or butter lettuce leaves, washed and dried

Instructions:

In a large skillet, heat olive oil over medium heat. Add the ground turkey and cook, breaking it apart with a spatula, until browned and cooked through.

Season the turkey with ground cumin, chili powder, garlic powder, onion powder, salt, and pepper. Stir well to incorporate the spices evenly.

Once the turkey is fully cooked and seasoned, remove the skillet from heat.

In a bowl, combine the halved cherry tomatoes, diced red onion, sliced avocado, lime juice, and chopped cilantro (if using). Toss gently to combine.

To assemble the lettuce wraps, spoon a portion of the seasoned turkey onto each lettuce leaf.

Top the turkey with the avocado and tomato mixture.

Serve the lettuce wraps immediately, allowing each person to customize their wraps with additional lime juice or cilantro if desired.

These Turkey and Avocado Lettuce Wraps are not only delicious but also low-carb and packed with protein. They make for a great lunch or light dinner option. Feel free to customize the toppings and seasonings according to your preferences.

Cauliflower Fried Rice

Ingredients:

- 1 medium-sized head of cauliflower, washed and dried
- 2 tablespoons vegetable oil or sesame oil
- 1 small onion, finely chopped
- 2 cloves garlic, minced
- 1 cup carrots, diced
- 1/2 cup peas (fresh or frozen)
- 2 eggs, beaten
- 3 tablespoons soy sauce (or tamari for a gluten-free option)
- 1 teaspoon ginger, grated (optional)
- 2 green onions, sliced for garnish
- Sesame seeds for garnish (optional)

Instructions:

Cut the cauliflower into florets and place them in a food processor. Pulse until the cauliflower resembles rice-sized pieces. You can also use a box grater to achieve a similar result.
Heat vegetable or sesame oil in a large skillet or wok over medium heat.
Add the chopped onion and sauté until it becomes translucent, about 2-3 minutes.
Stir in the minced garlic and cook for an additional 1-2 minutes until fragrant.
Add the diced carrots and cook for another 3-4 minutes until they start to soften.
Push the vegetables to one side of the skillet and pour the beaten eggs into the other side. Scramble the eggs until cooked through.
Combine the scrambled eggs with the vegetables in the skillet.
Add the cauliflower rice to the skillet, stirring well to combine all the ingredients.
Pour the soy sauce over the cauliflower rice and stir to evenly distribute the sauce. Add grated ginger if desired.
Add the peas and continue to cook for an additional 5-7 minutes or until the cauliflower rice is tender but not mushy.
Taste and adjust the seasoning, adding more soy sauce if needed.
Garnish the cauliflower fried rice with sliced green onions and sesame seeds.

Serve hot and enjoy your delicious and low-carb Cauliflower Fried Rice! It's a great way to incorporate more vegetables into your meal while still enjoying the flavors of traditional fried rice.

Caprese Salad Skewers

Ingredients:

- Cherry tomatoes
- Fresh mozzarella balls (small)
- Fresh basil leaves
- Balsamic glaze
- Extra virgin olive oil
- Salt and pepper, to taste
- Wooden skewers or toothpicks

Instructions:

Rinse the cherry tomatoes and fresh basil leaves. Pat them dry with a paper towel.
Thread one cherry tomato onto the skewer or toothpick, followed by a fresh basil leaf and a mozzarella ball.
Repeat the pattern until you have a few Caprese Salad Skewers ready.
Arrange the skewers on a serving platter or dish.
Drizzle the skewers with balsamic glaze and extra virgin olive oil.
Sprinkle a pinch of salt and pepper over the skewers for added flavor.
Serve immediately, or refrigerate until ready to serve.

These Caprese Salad Skewers are not only visually appealing but also burst with fresh and vibrant flavors. They make a great appetizer for parties or a light and refreshing snack. Feel free to customize the recipe by adding a sprinkle of dried oregano or a touch of garlic powder for extra seasoning. Enjoy!

Dinner:

Baked Lemon Garlic Butter Salmon

Ingredients:

- 4 salmon fillets
- Salt and black pepper, to taste
- 4 tablespoons unsalted butter, melted
- 4 cloves garlic, minced
- Zest of 1 lemon
- Juice of 1 lemon
- 1 teaspoon dried oregano or thyme (optional)
- Fresh parsley, chopped, for garnish
- Lemon slices, for serving

Instructions:

- Preheat your oven to 400°F (200°C). Line a baking sheet with parchment paper or lightly grease it.
- Place the salmon fillets on the prepared baking sheet. Season each fillet with salt and black pepper.
- In a small bowl, mix together the melted butter, minced garlic, lemon zest, lemon juice, and dried oregano or thyme (if using).
- Spoon the lemon garlic butter mixture over each salmon fillet, ensuring they are well-coated.
- Bake in the preheated oven for 12-15 minutes, or until the salmon flakes easily with a fork. Cooking time may vary depending on the thickness of your salmon fillets.
- Once cooked, remove the salmon from the oven and garnish with fresh chopped parsley.
- Serve the Baked Lemon Garlic Butter Salmon with lemon slices on the side.

Enjoy this flavorful and nutritious dish with your favorite side dishes, such as steamed vegetables, quinoa, or a fresh green salad. The combination of lemon, garlic, and butter enhances the natural taste of the salmon, creating a delicious and satisfying meal.

Spaghetti Squash with Pesto and Cherry Tomatoes

Ingredients:

- 1 medium-sized spaghetti squash
- 1 cup cherry tomatoes, halved
- 1/2 cup freshly grated Parmesan cheese
- Salt and black pepper, to taste

For the Pesto:

- 2 cups fresh basil leaves, packed
- 1/2 cup pine nuts or walnuts
- 1/2 cup freshly grated Parmesan cheese
- 2 cloves garlic, minced
- 1/2 cup extra virgin olive oil
- Salt and black pepper, to taste

Instructions:

Preheat your oven to 375°F (190°C).
Cut the spaghetti squash in half lengthwise. Scoop out the seeds with a spoon.
Place the squash halves, cut side down, on a baking sheet. Bake in the preheated oven for 30-40 minutes or until the squash is tender when pierced with a fork.
While the squash is baking, prepare the pesto. In a food processor, combine the basil, pine nuts or walnuts, Parmesan cheese, and minced garlic. Pulse until finely chopped.
With the food processor running, slowly drizzle in the olive oil until the pesto reaches your desired consistency. Season with salt and black pepper to taste.
Once the spaghetti squash is cooked, use a fork to scrape the flesh into strands.
In a large bowl, toss the spaghetti squash strands with the pesto until well coated.
Add the halved cherry tomatoes and toss gently.
Sprinkle freshly grated Parmesan cheese over the top and season with additional salt and black pepper if needed.
Serve the spaghetti squash with pesto and cherry tomatoes immediately, garnished with extra basil or Parmesan if desired.

This dish is not only gluten-free and low-carb but also packed with flavor and nutrients. It makes for a satisfying and wholesome meal. Enjoy!

Cauliflower Crust Pizza

Ingredients:

For the Cauliflower Crust:

- 1 medium-sized cauliflower head, riced (about 4 cups)
- 1 egg
- 1 cup shredded mozzarella cheese
- 1 teaspoon dried oregano
- 1 teaspoon garlic powder
- Salt and black pepper, to taste

For Topping (Customize as per your preference):

- Tomato sauce
- Cheese (mozzarella, Parmesan, etc.)
- Vegetables (bell peppers, onions, mushrooms, cherry tomatoes, etc.)
- Cooked meats (pepperoni, cooked chicken, sausage, etc.)
- Fresh basil or other herbs for garnish

Instructions:

Preheat your oven to 425°F (220°C). Place a pizza stone or a baking sheet in the oven while it's preheating.

Rice the cauliflower by removing the stem and leaves and then using a food processor to pulse the cauliflower florets until they resemble rice.

Place the riced cauliflower in a microwave-safe bowl and microwave on high for about 4-5 minutes. Allow it to cool for a few minutes.

Once the cauliflower is cool, transfer it to a clean kitchen towel or cheesecloth. Squeeze out as much moisture as possible. This step is crucial to getting a crispy crust.

In a bowl, combine the drained cauliflower, egg, shredded mozzarella cheese, oregano, garlic powder, salt, and black pepper. Mix well to form a dough-like consistency.

Place parchment paper on a pizza peel or another baking sheet. Spread the cauliflower dough onto the parchment paper, forming a round pizza crust.

Carefully transfer the parchment paper with the crust onto the preheated pizza stone or baking sheet in the oven.

Bake the crust for 12-15 minutes or until golden brown and firm.

Remove the crust from the oven and add your desired pizza toppings. Start with tomato sauce, cheese, vegetables, and meats.

Place the pizza back in the oven and bake for an additional 10-15 minutes or until the cheese is melted and bubbly.

Once done, remove the cauliflower crust pizza from the oven and let it cool for a few minutes. Slice and garnish with fresh basil or herbs.

Enjoy your homemade cauliflower crust pizza! It's a tasty and healthy alternative that allows you to indulge in pizza while reducing your carb intake.

Shrimp Stir-Fry with Vegetables

Ingredients:

- 1 lb (450g) large shrimp, peeled and deveined
- 2 cups broccoli florets
- 1 bell pepper, thinly sliced
- 1 carrot, julienned
- 1 cup snap peas, trimmed
- 3 cloves garlic, minced
- 1 tablespoon ginger, grated
- 3 tablespoons soy sauce
- 1 tablespoon oyster sauce
- 1 tablespoon cornstarch
- 2 tablespoons water
- 1 tablespoon sesame oil
- 2 tablespoons vegetable oil (for stir-frying)
- Cooked rice or noodles for serving

Instructions:

In a small bowl, mix soy sauce, oyster sauce, cornstarch, water, and sesame oil to create the stir-fry sauce. Set aside.
Heat vegetable oil in a wok or large skillet over medium-high heat.
Add minced garlic and grated ginger to the hot oil, stir-frying for about 30 seconds or until fragrant.
Add the shrimp to the wok and cook for 2-3 minutes or until they turn pink and opaque. Remove the shrimp from the wok and set aside.
In the same wok, add a bit more oil if needed. Stir-fry the broccoli, bell pepper, carrot, and snap peas for about 3-4 minutes or until they are slightly tender but still crisp.
Return the cooked shrimp to the wok with the vegetables.
Pour the prepared sauce over the shrimp and vegetables. Stir well to coat everything evenly and allow the sauce to thicken.
Cook for an additional 1-2 minutes until the shrimp are heated through, and the vegetables are coated in the sauce.
Taste and adjust the seasoning if necessary.
Serve the shrimp stir-fry over cooked rice or noodles.

Garnish with sliced green onions or sesame seeds if desired. This shrimp stir-fry with vegetables is not only delicious but also versatile—feel free to customize it by adding your favorite vegetables or adjusting the sauce according to your taste preferences. Enjoy your homemade shrimp stir-fry!

Eggplant Lasagna

Ingredients:

- 2 large eggplants, thinly sliced lengthwise
- 1 lb (450g) ground beef or ground turkey
- 1 onion, finely chopped
- 3 cloves garlic, minced
- 1 can (28 oz) crushed tomatoes
- 1 can (6 oz) tomato paste
- 1 teaspoon dried oregano
- 1 teaspoon dried basil
- Salt and black pepper, to taste
- 2 cups ricotta cheese
- 1 large egg
- 2 cups shredded mozzarella cheese
- 1/2 cup grated Parmesan cheese
- Fresh basil or parsley for garnish

Instructions:

Preheat your oven to 375°F (190°C).
Place the thinly sliced eggplant on a baking sheet. Sprinkle with salt and let it sit for about 15-20 minutes to draw out excess moisture. Afterward, pat the eggplant slices dry with paper towels.
In a large skillet, cook the ground beef or turkey over medium heat until browned. Add the chopped onion and minced garlic, cooking until the onion is softened.
Stir in the crushed tomatoes, tomato paste, dried oregano, dried basil, salt, and black pepper. Simmer the sauce for about 15-20 minutes, allowing the flavors to meld.
In a bowl, mix the ricotta cheese with the egg until well combined.
Assemble the lasagna layers in a baking dish. Start by spreading a layer of the meat sauce at the bottom.
Arrange a layer of eggplant slices on top of the sauce.
Spread half of the ricotta mixture over the eggplant layer.
Sprinkle a layer of shredded mozzarella cheese on top.
Repeat the process with another layer of meat sauce, eggplant slices, ricotta mixture, and mozzarella cheese.

Finish with a final layer of meat sauce and sprinkle grated Parmesan cheese on top.

Cover the baking dish with aluminum foil and bake in the preheated oven for 40-45 minutes. Remove the foil for the last 10-15 minutes to allow the top to brown.

Once the eggplant lasagna is cooked through and bubbly, remove it from the oven and let it rest for about 10 minutes before slicing.

Garnish with fresh basil or parsley before serving.

Enjoy your delicious and hearty eggplant lasagna! This dish is not only satisfying but also a great way to incorporate more vegetables into your meal.

Snacks:

Guacamole with Veggie Sticks

Guacamole Ingredients:

- 3 ripe avocados, peeled and pitted
- 1 small red onion, finely diced
- 1-2 tomatoes, diced
- 1 jalapeño pepper, seeded and finely chopped (optional, for heat)
- 1/4 cup fresh cilantro, chopped
- Juice of 1-2 limes
- Salt and pepper, to taste

Veggie Sticks:

- Carrot sticks
- Cucumber sticks
- Bell pepper strips (red, yellow, or green)
- Celery sticks

Instructions:

In a medium-sized bowl, mash the ripe avocados using a fork or potato masher. Leave some chunks for texture.
Add the finely diced red onion, diced tomatoes, chopped jalapeño (if using), and fresh cilantro to the mashed avocados.
Squeeze the juice of 1-2 limes into the mixture, depending on your taste preference. Mix well to combine.
Season the guacamole with salt and pepper to taste. Adjust the lime juice and seasoning as needed.
Cover the guacamole with plastic wrap, ensuring it touches the surface to prevent browning. Refrigerate for at least 30 minutes to let the flavors meld.
While the guacamole is chilling, prepare the veggie sticks. Wash and cut carrots, cucumber, bell peppers, and celery into sticks.
Once the guacamole is ready, give it a final stir and taste for seasoning.
Serve the guacamole in a bowl surrounded by the assorted veggie sticks.

Enjoy your guacamole with veggie sticks as a healthy and satisfying snack or appetizer. The creamy texture of the guacamole pairs perfectly with the crispness of the fresh vegetables, creating a delightful combination of flavors and textures.

Parmesan Crisps

Ingredients:

- 1 cup freshly grated Parmesan cheese

Optional Add-ins:

- Black pepper
- Dried herbs (such as thyme or rosemary)
- Red pepper flakes

Instructions:

> Preheat your oven to 375°F (190°C). Line a baking sheet with parchment paper.
> Place small mounds (about 1 tablespoon each) of grated Parmesan cheese on the prepared baking sheet, leaving enough space between them as they will spread during baking.
> Flatten and shape each mound into a thin, even circle using the back of a spoon.
> If desired, sprinkle the Parmesan circles with black pepper, dried herbs, or red pepper flakes for added flavor.
> Bake in the preheated oven for 5-7 minutes or until the edges are golden brown and the cheese is crispy.
> Remove the baking sheet from the oven and let the Parmesan crisps cool for a few minutes on the pan. They will continue to firm up as they cool.
> Carefully transfer the Parmesan crisps to a wire rack to cool completely.
> Once cooled and fully hardened, store the Parmesan crisps in an airtight container.

Enjoy these Parmesan crisps as a snack or use them to add a crunchy element to your salads or soups. Feel free to experiment with different herbs and spices to customize the flavor to your liking.

Deviled Eggs

Ingredients:

- 6 large eggs
- 3 tablespoons mayonnaise
- 1 teaspoon Dijon mustard
- 1 teaspoon white vinegar
- Salt and pepper, to taste
- Paprika or fresh herbs for garnish (optional)

Instructions:

Boiling the Eggs:
- Place the eggs in a single layer at the bottom of a saucepan or pot.
- Add enough water to the pot to cover the eggs by about an inch.
- Bring the water to a boil over medium-high heat.
- Once boiling, reduce the heat to low, cover, and let the eggs simmer for about 9-12 minutes.
- After the cooking time, transfer the eggs to an ice water bath to cool quickly.

Peeling the Eggs:
- Once the eggs are cool, gently tap them on a hard surface to crack the shell, then roll them to loosen.
- Peel the eggs under running water to help remove any small shell fragments.

Preparing the Filling:
- Cut the peeled eggs in half lengthwise.
- Carefully remove the yolks and place them in a bowl.
- Mash the yolks with a fork until they are crumbly.

Making the Deviled Egg Filling:
- Add mayonnaise, Dijon mustard, white vinegar, salt, and pepper to the mashed yolks.
- Mix until smooth and well combined. Adjust the seasoning to taste.

Filling the Eggs:
- Spoon or pipe the yolk mixture back into the egg white halves. You can use a pastry bag or a plastic sandwich bag with the corner snipped off for piping.

Garnishing:

- Sprinkle the filled deviled eggs with paprika or garnish with fresh herbs if desired.

Chilling:
- Refrigerate the deviled eggs for at least 30 minutes before serving to allow the flavors to meld.

Serve:
- Arrange the deviled eggs on a serving platter and enjoy!

Deviled eggs are a versatile dish, and you can customize the filling with additional ingredients like minced herbs, pickles, or a dash of hot sauce for extra flavor. They make for an excellent appetizer for any occasion.

Buffalo Cauliflower Bites

Ingredients:

For the Cauliflower Bites:

- 1 medium-sized head of cauliflower, cut into florets
- 1 cup all-purpose flour (or almond flour for a gluten-free option)
- 1 cup milk (or plant-based milk for a vegan option)
- 1 teaspoon garlic powder
- 1 teaspoon onion powder
- 1/2 teaspoon smoked paprika
- Salt and pepper, to taste

For the Buffalo Sauce:

- 1/2 cup hot sauce (such as Frank's RedHot)
- 1/4 cup unsalted butter (or vegan butter for a vegan option)
- 1 tablespoon white vinegar
- 1/2 teaspoon garlic powder
- 1/2 teaspoon Worcestershire sauce (optional, omit for a vegetarian/vegan version)
- Celery sticks and ranch or blue cheese dressing for serving

Instructions:

Preheat the Oven:
- Preheat your oven to 450°F (230°C).
- Line a baking sheet with parchment paper.

Prepare the Batter:
- In a bowl, whisk together the flour, milk, garlic powder, onion powder, smoked paprika, salt, and pepper until you have a smooth batter.

Coat the Cauliflower:
- Dip each cauliflower floret into the batter, ensuring it's evenly coated, then shake off any excess batter.

Bake the Cauliflower:
- Place the coated cauliflower florets on the prepared baking sheet.
- Bake in the preheated oven for 20-25 minutes or until the cauliflower is golden brown and crispy.

Prepare the Buffalo Sauce:
- While the cauliflower is baking, prepare the buffalo sauce. In a saucepan over medium heat, melt the butter. Add the hot sauce, white vinegar, garlic powder, and Worcestershire sauce (if using). Stir until well combined. Simmer for a couple of minutes, then remove from heat.

Coat the Cauliflower with Buffalo Sauce:
- Once the cauliflower is done baking, transfer it to a large bowl.
- Pour the buffalo sauce over the cauliflower and toss until each piece is well coated.

Serve:
- Arrange the buffalo cauliflower bites on a serving platter.
- Serve with celery sticks and your choice of ranch or blue cheese dressing.

These Buffalo Cauliflower Bites are a crowd-pleaser and a great appetizer or snack for game day or any gathering. Adjust the level of heat in the buffalo sauce according to your preference, and enjoy the spicy, tangy goodness of this cauliflower dish!

Cucumber and Cream Cheese Bites

Ingredients:

- 1 large cucumber, washed and sliced into rounds
- 8 ounces (225g) cream cheese, softened
- 2 tablespoons fresh dill, chopped
- 1 tablespoon chives, finely chopped (optional)
- Salt and black pepper, to taste
- Cherry tomatoes or smoked salmon for garnish (optional)

Instructions:

Prepare the Cucumbers:
- Wash the cucumber and cut it into thin rounds, about 1/4 inch thick. You can peel the cucumber if you prefer, but leaving the skin on adds color and texture.

Prepare the Cream Cheese Mixture:
- In a bowl, mix the softened cream cheese, chopped fresh dill, chives (if using), salt, and black pepper. Stir until well combined.

Assemble the Bites:
- Place a small dollop of the cream cheese mixture on each cucumber round.

Garnish (Optional):
- If desired, garnish each bite with a small piece of cherry tomato or a slice of smoked salmon. This adds color and additional flavor.

Serve:
- Arrange the cucumber and cream cheese bites on a serving platter.

Chill (Optional):
- For a cooler and firmer texture, you can refrigerate the bites for 15-30 minutes before serving.

Enjoy:
- Serve these refreshing bites at your next gathering or enjoy them as a light snack.

These Cucumber and Cream Cheese Bites are not only easy to prepare but also offer a crisp, cool, and creamy combination that's sure to be a hit. Feel free to customize the recipe by adding your favorite herbs or experimenting with different garnishes.

Sides:

Roasted Brussels Sprouts with Bacon

Ingredients:

- 1 lb (450g) Brussels sprouts, trimmed and halved
- 4-6 slices of bacon, chopped
- 2 tablespoons olive oil
- Salt and black pepper, to taste
- 1-2 tablespoons balsamic vinegar (optional, for drizzling)

Instructions:

Preheat the Oven:
- Preheat your oven to 400°F (200°C).

Prepare Brussels Sprouts:
- Trim the ends of the Brussels sprouts and cut them in half.

Cook Bacon:
- In a large oven-safe skillet, cook the chopped bacon over medium heat until it becomes crispy. Remove excess bacon fat, leaving about 1-2 tablespoons in the skillet.

Combine with Brussels Sprouts:
- Add the halved Brussels sprouts to the skillet with the bacon and bacon fat. Drizzle with olive oil, and toss until the Brussels sprouts are evenly coated.

Season:
- Season the Brussels sprouts with salt and black pepper to taste. Toss again to ensure even seasoning.

Roast in the Oven:
- Place the skillet in the preheated oven and roast for 20-25 minutes or until the Brussels sprouts are caramelized and crispy on the edges. Stir halfway through cooking for even roasting.

Finish and Serve:
- Once roasted, remove the skillet from the oven. If desired, drizzle with balsamic vinegar for extra flavor.

Serve Hot:
- Transfer the roasted Brussels sprouts and bacon to a serving dish and serve hot.

These Roasted Brussels Sprouts with Bacon make a delicious side dish for any meal. The combination of crispy bacon and caramelized Brussels sprouts provides a delightful contrast of textures and flavors. Enjoy!

Garlic Butter Asparagus

Ingredients:

- 1 lb (450g) fresh asparagus, woody ends trimmed
- 2 tablespoons unsalted butter
- 3 cloves garlic, minced
- Salt and black pepper, to taste
- Fresh lemon wedges for serving (optional)

Instructions:

- Prepare Asparagus:
    - Trim the woody ends from the asparagus spears. You can snap them off or cut them about 1-2 inches from the bottom.
- Saute Garlic:
    - In a large skillet, melt the butter over medium heat. Add the minced garlic and sauté for about 1-2 minutes, or until the garlic becomes fragrant. Be careful not to brown the garlic too much.
- Cook Asparagus:
    - Add the trimmed asparagus to the skillet, tossing to coat them evenly with the garlic butter.
- Season:
    - Season the asparagus with salt and black pepper to taste. Continue cooking, stirring occasionally, until the asparagus is tender but still has a slight crispness. This usually takes about 5-7 minutes, depending on the thickness of the asparagus.
- Serve:
    - Transfer the garlic butter asparagus to a serving dish.
- Optional Garnish:
    - Squeeze fresh lemon juice over the asparagus just before serving for a bright and citrusy flavor (optional).
- Serve Hot:
    - Serve the Garlic Butter Asparagus hot as a delightful side dish.

This simple yet flavorful recipe is perfect for showcasing the natural sweetness of asparagus while adding a rich garlic butter element. It pairs well with a variety of main dishes and makes for an excellent addition to your dinner table. Enjoy!

Creamy Cauliflower Mash

Ingredients:

- 1 large head of cauliflower, cut into florets
- 2 cloves garlic, minced
- 2 tablespoons butter
- 1/4 cup heavy cream (or milk for a lighter version)
- Salt and black pepper, to taste
- Chopped fresh chives or parsley for garnish (optional)

Instructions:

Steam or Boil Cauliflower:
- Place the cauliflower florets in a steamer basket and steam until tender. Alternatively, you can boil the cauliflower in a pot of water until fork-tender. This usually takes about 10-15 minutes.

Drain and Dry:
- Once the cauliflower is cooked, drain any excess water and pat the florets dry with a paper towel. Removing excess moisture is essential for achieving a creamy consistency.

Blend or Mash:
- In a food processor or using a hand blender, blend the cauliflower until smooth. If you prefer a chunkier texture, you can use a potato masher.

Add Butter and Garlic:
- In a saucepan over medium heat, melt the butter. Add the minced garlic and sauté for about 1-2 minutes, or until fragrant.

Combine with Cauliflower:
- Add the cauliflower puree to the saucepan with the melted butter and garlic. Stir to combine.

Add Cream:
- Pour in the heavy cream (or milk) and continue stirring until the mixture is well combined and reaches your desired creamy consistency.

Season:
- Season the creamy cauliflower mash with salt and black pepper to taste. Adjust the seasoning as needed.

Garnish and Serve:
- If desired, garnish with chopped fresh chives or parsley before serving.

Enjoy:

- Serve the creamy cauliflower mash hot as a side dish. It pairs well with a variety of main courses.

This creamy cauliflower mash is a versatile and satisfying side dish that complements many meals. It's a great option for those looking to reduce their carbohydrate intake while still enjoying a comforting and flavorful dish.

Sauteed Green Beans with Almonds

Ingredients:

- 1 lb (450g) fresh green beans, trimmed
- 2 tablespoons olive oil
- 2 cloves garlic, minced
- 1/3 cup sliced almonds
- Salt and black pepper, to taste
- Lemon wedges for serving (optional)

Instructions:

Blanch Green Beans:
- Bring a large pot of salted water to a boil. Add the trimmed green beans and cook for 2-3 minutes or until they are bright green and slightly tender. Drain the green beans and immediately transfer them to a bowl of ice water to stop the cooking process. Once cooled, drain them again and pat dry.

Saute Garlic and Almonds:
- In a large skillet, heat olive oil over medium heat. Add minced garlic and sauté for about 1 minute until fragrant. Be careful not to brown the garlic.

Add Green Beans:
- Add the blanched green beans to the skillet, tossing them to coat evenly with the garlic-infused oil.

Saute and Toast Almonds:
- Add the sliced almonds to the skillet with the green beans. Continue sautéing for 3-4 minutes, stirring occasionally, until the green beans are crisp-tender and the almonds are toasted.

Season:
- Season the sautéed green beans and almonds with salt and black pepper to taste. Adjust the seasoning as needed.

Serve:
- Transfer the green beans and almonds to a serving dish.

Optional Garnish:
- If desired, squeeze fresh lemon juice over the green beans just before serving for a burst of citrus flavor.

Enjoy:
- Serve the sautéed green beans with almonds hot as a flavorful side dish.

This dish is not only tasty but also visually appealing with the vibrant green beans and the crunch of the toasted almonds. It makes a wonderful accompaniment to a variety of main courses.

Jicama Fries with Chipotle Mayo

Ingredients:

For Jicama Fries:

- 1 large jicama, peeled and cut into matchstick-sized fries
- 2 tablespoons olive oil
- 1 teaspoon paprika
- 1 teaspoon garlic powder
- 1/2 teaspoon cumin
- Salt and black pepper, to taste

For Chipotle Mayo:

- 1/2 cup mayonnaise
- 1-2 teaspoons adobo sauce from canned chipotle peppers (adjust to taste)
- 1 teaspoon lime juice
- Salt and black pepper, to taste

Instructions:

Jicama Fries:

Preheat Oven:
- Preheat your oven to 425°F (220°C).

Prepare Jicama:
- Peel the jicama and cut it into matchstick-sized fries.

Season Fries:
- In a large bowl, toss the jicama fries with olive oil, paprika, garlic powder, cumin, salt, and black pepper until well coated.

Spread on Baking Sheet:
- Arrange the seasoned jicama fries in a single layer on a baking sheet lined with parchment paper.

Bake:
- Bake in the preheated oven for 25-30 minutes or until the fries are golden brown and crispy, flipping them halfway through cooking.

Chipotle Mayo:
- In a small bowl, mix together mayonnaise, adobo sauce, lime juice, salt, and black pepper. Adjust the adobo sauce to achieve your desired level of spiciness.

Serve:
- Serve the jicama fries hot with a side of chipotle mayo for dipping.

Enjoy:
- Enjoy this delicious and healthier snack!

These jicama fries with chipotle mayo are a flavorful and satisfying alternative to traditional french fries. The chipotle mayo adds a smoky and spicy kick, complementing the crispiness of the jicama fries. They make a great appetizer, side dish, or snack for any occasion.

Desserts:

Keto Chocolate Avocado Pudding

Ingredients:

- 2 ripe avocados, peeled and pitted
- 1/4 cup unsweetened cocoa powder
- 1/4 cup almond milk (or any low-carb milk of your choice)
- 1/4 cup powdered erythritol or sweetener of choice
- 1 teaspoon vanilla extract
- A pinch of salt

Optional Toppings:

- Whipped cream
- Chopped nuts
- Shredded coconut

Instructions:

Blend Avocados:
- In a blender or food processor, combine the ripe avocados, cocoa powder, almond milk, powdered erythritol, vanilla extract, and a pinch of salt.

Blend Until Smooth:
- Blend the ingredients until smooth and creamy. Scrape down the sides of the blender or food processor as needed to ensure everything is well combined.

Adjust Sweetness:
- Taste the pudding and adjust the sweetness if needed by adding more sweetener according to your preference.

Chill:
- Transfer the chocolate avocado pudding to a bowl or individual serving dishes and refrigerate for at least 30 minutes to allow it to chill and set.

Serve:
- Once chilled, serve the keto chocolate avocado pudding on its own or with optional toppings like whipped cream, chopped nuts, or shredded coconut.

Enjoy:

- Enjoy this decadent and keto-friendly dessert!

This chocolate avocado pudding is not only suitable for those following a keto diet but is also a great option for anyone looking for a healthier dessert alternative. The avocado provides a creamy texture, and the cocoa powder adds a rich chocolate flavor without the added sugars. It's a delicious treat that satisfies sweet cravings while staying low in carbohydrates.

Almond Flour Chocolate Chip Cookies

Ingredients:

- 2 cups almond flour
- 1/2 cup unsalted butter, softened
- 1/2 cup granulated erythritol or sweetener of choice
- 1 large egg
- 1 teaspoon vanilla extract
- 1/2 teaspoon baking soda
- 1/4 teaspoon salt
- 1/2 cup sugar-free chocolate chips

Instructions:

Preheat Oven:
- Preheat your oven to 350°F (175°C). Line a baking sheet with parchment paper.

Cream Butter and Sweetener:
- In a large bowl, cream together the softened butter and granulated erythritol (or sweetener of choice) until smooth.

Add Egg and Vanilla:
- Add the egg and vanilla extract to the butter mixture. Beat until well combined.

Combine Dry Ingredients:
- In a separate bowl, whisk together the almond flour, baking soda, and salt.

Mix Wet and Dry Ingredients:
- Gradually add the dry ingredients to the wet ingredients, mixing until a cookie dough forms.

Fold in Chocolate Chips:
- Gently fold in the sugar-free chocolate chips until evenly distributed throughout the cookie dough.

Shape Cookies:
- Scoop tablespoon-sized portions of cookie dough and roll them into balls. Place them on the prepared baking sheet, leaving enough space between each cookie.

Flatten Cookies (Optional):
- If you prefer flatter cookies, you can gently flatten each cookie with the back of a fork or your fingers.

Bake:
- Bake in the preheated oven for 10-12 minutes or until the edges are golden brown.

Cool:
- Allow the cookies to cool on the baking sheet for a few minutes before transferring them to a wire rack to cool completely.

Enjoy:
- Once cooled, enjoy your almond flour chocolate chip cookies!

These cookies are not only delicious but also grain-free and low in carbs, making them a great option for those following a gluten-free or keto lifestyle. Adjust the sweetness to your liking and savor the rich flavors of almond flour and sugar-free chocolate chips.

Berry Coconut Chia Seed Popsicles

Ingredients:

- 1 cup mixed berries (strawberries, blueberries, raspberries)
- 1 can (13.5 oz) coconut milk (full-fat for creamier popsicles)
- 2-3 tablespoons honey or maple syrup (adjust to taste)
- 1 teaspoon vanilla extract
- 2 tablespoons chia seeds

Instructions:

Prepare the Berries:
- Wash and hull the strawberries if using. If the berries are large, you can chop them into smaller pieces.

Blend Ingredients:
- In a blender, combine the mixed berries, coconut milk, honey or maple syrup, and vanilla extract. Blend until smooth.

Add Chia Seeds:
- Stir in the chia seeds into the blended mixture. Make sure the chia seeds are evenly distributed.

Let the Mixture Sit:
- Allow the mixture to sit for about 10-15 minutes to let the chia seeds absorb some of the liquid. This will help thicken the mixture.

Fill Popsicle Molds:
- Pour the berry coconut chia seed mixture into popsicle molds.

Insert Sticks:
- Insert popsicle sticks into each mold, making sure they are centered.

Freeze:
- Place the popsicle molds in the freezer and let them freeze for at least 4-6 hours, or until completely set.

Unmold and Enjoy:
- Once the popsicles are fully frozen, remove them from the molds. If they are a bit stubborn, you can briefly run the molds under warm water to help release the popsicles.

Serve and Enjoy:
- Enjoy your Berry Coconut Chia Seed Popsicles on a hot day!

These popsicles are not only a tasty and cool treat but also offer the added nutritional benefits of chia seeds and antioxidant-rich berries. Feel free to customize the recipe by using your favorite combination of berries or adjusting the sweetness to your liking.

Lemon Cheesecake Fat Bombs

Ingredients:

- 8 oz (225g) cream cheese, softened
- 1/4 cup unsalted butter, softened
- 1/4 cup coconut oil, melted
- Zest of 1 lemon
- 2 tablespoons fresh lemon juice
- 1/4 cup powdered erythritol or sweetener of choice
- 1 teaspoon vanilla extract
- Pinch of salt

Optional Coating:

- Unsweetened shredded coconut
- Lemon zest

Instructions:

Prepare Ingredients:
- Allow the cream cheese and butter to soften to room temperature for easier mixing.

Mix Cream Cheese and Butter:
- In a bowl, combine the softened cream cheese and butter. Use a hand mixer or stand mixer to beat them together until smooth and creamy.

Add Remaining Ingredients:
- Add the melted coconut oil, lemon zest, fresh lemon juice, powdered erythritol, vanilla extract, and a pinch of salt to the cream cheese mixture. Mix until well combined.

Taste and Adjust:
- Taste the mixture and adjust the sweetness or lemon flavor according to your preference.

Chill Mixture:
- Place the mixture in the refrigerator for about 30 minutes to firm up slightly.

Shape Fat Bombs:

- Once the mixture has firmed up, use a spoon or a cookie scoop to shape small balls (fat bombs) and place them on a parchment paper-lined tray.

Optional Coating:
- If desired, roll the fat bombs in unsweetened shredded coconut or lemon zest for an extra layer of flavor and texture.

Chill Again:
- Place the fat bombs in the refrigerator for at least 1-2 hours or until they are firm.

Serve and Enjoy:
- Once chilled, these lemon cheesecake fat bombs are ready to be enjoyed. Store any leftovers in the refrigerator.

These fat bombs are a delicious way to increase your healthy fat intake while staying low in carbs. The lemon flavor adds a refreshing twist, making them a perfect treat for those moments when you need a quick energy boost or a satisfying dessert on a ketogenic diet.

Dark Chocolate Dipped Strawberries

Ingredients:

- Fresh strawberries, washed and dried
- 6-8 ounces (170-225g) dark chocolate, chopped
- 1 tablespoon coconut oil (optional, for smoother chocolate)
- Toppings of your choice: chopped nuts, shredded coconut, sea salt, etc.

Instructions:

Prepare Strawberries:
- Wash and thoroughly dry the strawberries. It's important that they are completely dry to help the chocolate adhere.

Melt Chocolate:
- In a heatproof bowl, melt the dark chocolate. You can do this using a double boiler or by microwaving in 20-30 second intervals, stirring well between each interval. If desired, add coconut oil to the chocolate for a smoother consistency.

Dip Strawberries:
- Holding a strawberry by the green stem, dip it into the melted chocolate, swirling to coat as much of the berry as you desire.

Tap Off Excess:
- Allow any excess chocolate to drip off the strawberry back into the bowl.

Place on Parchment Paper:
- Place the dipped strawberries on a parchment paper-lined tray or plate.

Add Toppings (Optional):
- While the chocolate is still wet, you can sprinkle your favorite toppings over the strawberries. Popular choices include chopped nuts, shredded coconut, or a pinch of sea salt.

Let Chocolate Set:
- Allow the chocolate to set by placing the tray in the refrigerator for about 20-30 minutes.

Serve and Enjoy:
- Once the chocolate has hardened, your dark chocolate dipped strawberries are ready to be enjoyed.

These dark chocolate dipped strawberries make for a lovely dessert or a sweet treat for special occasions. The contrast between the sweet strawberries and the rich, slightly bitter dark chocolate is truly delightful. They are perfect for serving at parties or as a romantic and easy-to-make dessert.

Smoothies:

Green Keto Smoothie with Avocado and Spinach

Ingredients:

1/2 avocado, peeled and pitted

1 cup fresh spinach leaves

1/2 cup unsweetened almond milk (or any low-carb milk of your choice)

1/2 cup water

1/4 cup cucumber, peeled and chopped

1/4 cup celery, chopped

1/2 teaspoon grated ginger (optional)

1-2 tablespoons lemon juice

Ice cubes (optional)

Sweetener (such as stevia or erythritol), to taste (optional)

Instructions:

Prepare Ingredients:

Ensure the avocado is peeled and pitted. Chop the cucumber and celery into smaller pieces.

Combine Ingredients:

In a blender, combine the avocado, spinach, almond milk, water, cucumber, celery, grated ginger (if using), and lemon juice.

Blend Until Smooth:

Blend the ingredients until smooth and creamy. If the smoothie is too thick, you can add more water or almond milk to reach your desired consistency.

Taste and Adjust:

Taste the smoothie and adjust the sweetness if needed by adding a keto-friendly sweetener, such as stevia or erythritol.

Add Ice Cubes (Optional):

If you prefer a colder and icier smoothie, you can add a handful of ice cubes and blend again.

Pour and Serve:

Pour the green keto smoothie into a glass and serve immediately.

This green keto smoothie is not only low in carbs but also packed with healthy fats from the avocado, making it a satisfying and nutritious option. The spinach adds vitamins and minerals, while the cucumber and celery contribute a refreshing element. Adjust the ingredients and sweetness to fit your taste preferences and enjoy a delicious green smoothie that aligns with your keto lifestyle.

Berry and Broccoli Stir-Fry

Ingredients:

- 2 cups broccoli florets
- 1 cup mixed berries (strawberries, blueberries, raspberries)
- 1 tablespoon olive oil
- 2 cloves garlic, minced
- 1 tablespoon soy sauce or tamari (for a gluten-free option)
- 1 tablespoon balsamic vinegar
- 1 tablespoon honey or maple syrup
- Salt and pepper, to taste
- Sesame seeds for garnish (optional)

Instructions:

Blanch Broccoli:
- Bring a pot of water to a boil and blanch the broccoli florets for 2-3 minutes, or until they are slightly tender but still crisp. Drain and set aside.

Prepare Berry Sauce:
- In a small bowl, mix together the soy sauce or tamari, balsamic vinegar, and honey or maple syrup. Set aside.

Stir-Fry:
- In a large skillet or wok, heat olive oil over medium-high heat. Add minced garlic and sauté for about 30 seconds until fragrant.

Add Broccoli:
- Add the blanched broccoli florets to the skillet. Stir-fry for 2-3 minutes until they start to brown slightly.

Add Mixed Berries:
- Add the mixed berries to the skillet and stir-fry for an additional 1-2 minutes until the berries are heated through but still firm.

Pour Sauce:
- Pour the prepared sauce over the broccoli and berries. Toss everything together to coat the ingredients evenly.

Season:
- Season with salt and pepper to taste. Adjust the sweetness or acidity by adding more honey, if needed.

Garnish and Serve:

- Garnish with sesame seeds if desired and serve the berry and broccoli stir-fry immediately.

This unique stir-fry combines the sweetness of berries with the savory and slightly tangy flavors of the sauce. It's a colorful and vibrant dish that's not only tasty but also loaded with nutrients from both the berries and broccoli. Feel free to customize the recipe by adding your favorite nuts or protein source if you desire a heartier meal.

Cabbage and Ground Turkey Skillet

Ingredients:

- 1 lb (450g) ground turkey
- 1 small head of cabbage, thinly sliced
- 1 onion, finely chopped
- 2 cloves garlic, minced
- 1 can (14 oz) diced tomatoes (undrained)
- 1 teaspoon paprika
- 1/2 teaspoon dried oregano
- Salt and black pepper, to taste
- 2 tablespoons olive oil
- Fresh parsley, chopped (for garnish, optional)

Instructions:

Brown Ground Turkey:
- In a large skillet, heat olive oil over medium-high heat. Add ground turkey and cook until browned, breaking it apart with a spoon as it cooks.

Add Onion and Garlic:
- Add chopped onion and minced garlic to the skillet. Sauté for 2-3 minutes until the onion becomes translucent.

Add Cabbage:
- Add the thinly sliced cabbage to the skillet. Stir well to combine with the ground turkey, onion, and garlic.

Season:
- Sprinkle paprika, dried oregano, salt, and black pepper over the mixture. Stir to evenly distribute the seasonings.

Pour in Tomatoes:
- Pour the can of diced tomatoes with their juice into the skillet. Stir to combine.

Cover and Simmer:
- Cover the skillet and let the mixture simmer for about 15-20 minutes, or until the cabbage is tender.

Check Seasoning:
- Taste and adjust the seasoning if needed. Add more salt, pepper, or herbs to suit your preferences.

Garnish and Serve:

- Garnish with chopped fresh parsley if desired, then serve the cabbage and ground turkey skillet hot.

This skillet dish is not only flavorful but also low in carbs and high in protein, making it a great option for a wholesome and satisfying meal. Feel free to customize the recipe by adding your favorite herbs, spices, or additional vegetables for extra variety and nutrition.

Salmon and Avocado Salad

Ingredients:

For the Salmon:

- 2 salmon fillets
- 1 tablespoon olive oil
- Salt and black pepper, to taste
- Lemon wedges for serving

For the Salad:

- 4 cups mixed salad greens (e.g., spinach, arugula, or your choice)
- 1 ripe avocado, sliced
- 1 cup cherry tomatoes, halved
- 1/4 red onion, thinly sliced
- 1/4 cup cucumber, sliced
- 2 tablespoons extra virgin olive oil
- 1 tablespoon balsamic vinegar
- Salt and black pepper, to taste
- Fresh herbs (such as dill or parsley), for garnish (optional)

Instructions:

Cook the Salmon:
- Preheat the oven to 400°F (200°C). Place the salmon fillets on a baking sheet lined with parchment paper. Drizzle with olive oil and season with salt and black pepper. Bake for 12-15 minutes or until the salmon is cooked through and flakes easily. Squeeze lemon juice over the cooked salmon before serving.

Prepare the Salad:
- In a large bowl, combine the mixed salad greens, sliced avocado, cherry tomatoes, red onion, and cucumber.

Make the Dressing:
- In a small bowl, whisk together extra virgin olive oil and balsamic vinegar. Season with salt and black pepper to taste.

Assemble the Salad:
- Drizzle the dressing over the salad ingredients and toss gently to coat everything evenly.

Add Salmon:
- Break the cooked salmon into bite-sized pieces and add it to the salad.

Garnish and Serve:
- Garnish the salad with fresh herbs if desired. Serve immediately, and enjoy your salmon and avocado salad!

This salad is not only delicious but also packed with healthy fats, protein, and a variety of nutrients. It's a well-balanced and satisfying meal that's perfect for lunch or a light dinner. Feel free to customize the salad with your favorite vegetables or add a sprinkle of nuts or seeds for extra crunch.

Eggplant and Zucchini Gratin

Ingredients:

- 1 large eggplant, thinly sliced
- 2 medium zucchinis, thinly sliced
- 2 tablespoons olive oil
- 2 cloves garlic, minced
- 1 cup shredded mozzarella cheese
- 1/2 cup grated Parmesan cheese
- 1 cup tomato sauce or marinara sauce
- 1 teaspoon dried oregano
- 1 teaspoon dried basil
- Salt and black pepper, to taste
- Fresh basil or parsley for garnish (optional)

Instructions:

Preheat Oven:
- Preheat your oven to 375°F (190°C).

Prepare Vegetables:
- Slice the eggplant and zucchini into thin rounds. You can use a mandoline or a sharp knife for even slices.

Sauté Vegetables:
- In a large skillet, heat olive oil over medium heat. Add minced garlic and sauté for about 1 minute until fragrant. Add the sliced eggplant and zucchini. Cook for 5-7 minutes, stirring occasionally, until the vegetables are slightly softened. Season with salt and black pepper to taste.

Assemble Gratin:
- In a baking dish, spread a thin layer of tomato sauce. Arrange a layer of the sautéed eggplant and zucchini over the sauce. Sprinkle with a portion of mozzarella and Parmesan cheese. Repeat the layers until all the vegetables are used, finishing with a layer of cheese on top.

Season and Bake:
- Sprinkle dried oregano and dried basil over the top. Season with additional salt and black pepper if needed. Bake in the preheated oven for 25-30 minutes or until the cheese is melted and bubbly, and the vegetables are tender.

Garnish and Serve:
- Remove the gratin from the oven and let it cool for a few minutes. Garnish with fresh basil or parsley if desired. Slice and serve.

This eggplant and zucchini gratin is a delightful side dish or even a light vegetarian main course. The layers of vegetables, tomato sauce, and cheesy goodness create a comforting and satisfying dish. Enjoy it as a standalone meal or alongside your favorite protein.

Soups:

Tomato Basil Soup with Heavy Cream

Ingredients:

- 2 tablespoons olive oil
- 1 onion, finely chopped
- 2 cloves garlic, minced
- 2 cans (28 oz each) whole peeled tomatoes
- 1 can (14 oz) crushed tomatoes
- 1 cup fresh basil leaves, chopped
- 1 teaspoon dried oregano
- 1 teaspoon sugar (optional, to balance acidity)
- Salt and black pepper, to taste
- 1 cup heavy cream
- 2 tablespoons butter (optional, for added richness)
- Grated Parmesan cheese for garnish (optional)
- Fresh basil leaves for garnish (optional)

Instructions:

Sauté Onion and Garlic:
- In a large pot, heat olive oil over medium heat. Add finely chopped onion and sauté until softened, about 5 minutes. Add minced garlic and cook for an additional 1-2 minutes until fragrant.

Add Tomatoes:
- Add the whole peeled tomatoes and crushed tomatoes to the pot. Break up the whole tomatoes with a spoon or spatula. Stir in chopped fresh basil and dried oregano.

Season:
- Season with salt and black pepper to taste. If the tomatoes are too acidic, you can add a teaspoon of sugar to balance the flavors.

Simmer:
- Bring the soup to a simmer and let it cook for about 15-20 minutes, allowing the flavors to meld.

Blend:

- Use an immersion blender to blend the soup until smooth. Alternatively, carefully transfer the soup to a blender in batches and blend until smooth. Be cautious as the soup will be hot.

Add Heavy Cream and Butter:
- Return the blended soup to the pot. Stir in the heavy cream and butter (if using). Heat the soup gently, but do not bring it to a boil.

Adjust Seasoning:
- Taste the soup and adjust the seasoning as needed. If you prefer a thinner consistency, you can add more cream or broth.

Serve:
- Ladle the creamy tomato basil soup into bowls. Garnish with grated Parmesan cheese and fresh basil leaves if desired. Serve hot.

This creamy tomato basil soup is a classic comfort food with the added richness of heavy cream. It pairs well with a crusty baguette or a grilled cheese sandwich. Enjoy the delicious flavors and warmth of this comforting soup!

Cabbage and Sausage Soup

Ingredients:

- 1 lb (450g) smoked sausage or kielbasa, sliced
- 1 onion, diced
- 2 carrots, peeled and sliced
- 2 celery stalks, sliced
- 3 cloves garlic, minced
- 1 small head cabbage, chopped
- 1 can (14 oz) diced tomatoes
- 6 cups chicken or vegetable broth
- 1 teaspoon dried thyme
- 1 teaspoon dried oregano
- Salt and black pepper, to taste
- 1 bay leaf
- 2 tablespoons olive oil
- Fresh parsley for garnish (optional)

Instructions:

Sauté Sausage:
- In a large pot or Dutch oven, heat olive oil over medium heat. Add sliced sausage and cook until browned. Remove the sausage from the pot and set aside.

Sauté Vegetables:
- In the same pot, add diced onion, sliced carrots, sliced celery, and minced garlic. Sauté for about 5 minutes until the vegetables are softened.

Add Cabbage:
- Add the chopped cabbage to the pot and cook for an additional 5 minutes until it starts to wilt.

Combine Ingredients:
- Return the browned sausage to the pot. Add diced tomatoes (with their juice), chicken or vegetable broth, dried thyme, dried oregano, salt, black pepper, and the bay leaf.

Simmer:
- Bring the soup to a simmer, then reduce the heat to low. Cover and let it simmer for about 20-30 minutes, or until the vegetables are tender.

Adjust Seasoning:
- Taste the soup and adjust the seasoning if needed. Remove the bay leaf before serving.

Serve:
- Ladle the cabbage and sausage soup into bowls. Garnish with fresh parsley if desired. Serve hot and enjoy!

This cabbage and sausage soup is not only delicious but also filling and nutritious. It's a great option for a satisfying meal, especially during colder months. Feel free to customize the recipe by adding your favorite herbs or spices to suit your taste preferences.

Creamy Broccoli and Cheese Soup

Ingredients:

- 4 cups broccoli florets
- 1 onion, finely chopped
- 2 carrots, peeled and diced
- 2 celery stalks, diced
- 3 cups chicken or vegetable broth
- 2 cups sharp cheddar cheese, shredded
- 1 cup whole milk or half-and-half
- 1/3 cup all-purpose flour
- 1/4 cup unsalted butter
- 2 cloves garlic, minced
- 1/2 teaspoon dried thyme
- Salt and black pepper, to taste
- Pinch of nutmeg (optional)
- Croutons or additional shredded cheese for garnish (optional)

Instructions:

Prepare Vegetables:
- In a large pot, melt butter over medium heat. Add chopped onion, diced carrots, and diced celery. Sauté for 5-7 minutes until the vegetables are softened.

Add Garlic and Flour:
- Add minced garlic and sauté for an additional 1-2 minutes until fragrant. Sprinkle flour over the vegetables and stir well to coat.

Make Roux:
- Cook the flour and vegetable mixture (roux) for 2-3 minutes, stirring constantly to avoid burning.

Add Broth:
- Slowly whisk in the chicken or vegetable broth to the roux, ensuring there are no lumps. Bring the mixture to a simmer.

Cook Broccoli:
- Add the broccoli florets and dried thyme to the pot. Simmer for about 15 minutes or until the broccoli is tender.

Blend Soup:

- Use an immersion blender to blend the soup to your desired consistency. Alternatively, transfer a portion of the soup to a blender and blend until smooth, then return it to the pot.

Add Cheese and Milk:
- Stir in shredded cheddar cheese until melted. Pour in whole milk or half-and-half, stirring continuously.

Season:
- Season the soup with salt, black pepper, and a pinch of nutmeg if using. Adjust the seasoning to taste.

Simmer:
- Allow the soup to simmer for an additional 5-10 minutes, allowing the flavors to meld.

Serve:
- Ladle the creamy broccoli and cheese soup into bowls. Garnish with croutons or additional shredded cheese if desired. Serve hot and enjoy!

This homemade broccoli and cheese soup is a classic comfort food that's both creamy and satisfying. It's a great way to enjoy the goodness of broccoli with the rich flavor of cheddar cheese. Feel free to customize the recipe by adding your favorite herbs or spices.

Chicken Zoodle Soup

Ingredients:

- 1 tablespoon olive oil
- 1 onion, finely chopped
- 2 carrots, peeled and sliced
- 2 celery stalks, sliced
- 3 cloves garlic, minced
- 8 cups chicken broth
- 2 cups cooked shredded chicken (rotisserie chicken works well)
- 2 medium zucchinis, spiralized into noodles
- 1 teaspoon dried thyme
- 1 teaspoon dried oregano
- Salt and black pepper, to taste
- Fresh parsley, chopped, for garnish (optional)
- Lemon wedges, for serving (optional)

Instructions:

Sauté Vegetables:
- In a large pot, heat olive oil over medium heat. Add chopped onion, sliced carrots, sliced celery, and minced garlic. Sauté for about 5-7 minutes until the vegetables are softened.

Add Broth:
- Pour in the chicken broth and bring the mixture to a simmer.

Add Chicken:
- Stir in the shredded cooked chicken, dried thyme, and dried oregano. Let the soup simmer for an additional 10-15 minutes to allow the flavors to meld.

Add Zucchini Noodles:
- Add the spiralized zucchini noodles to the pot. Cook for about 2-3 minutes until the zoodles are just tender. Be careful not to overcook, as zucchini noodles can become mushy quickly.

Season:
- Season the soup with salt and black pepper to taste. Adjust the seasoning as needed.

Serve:

- Ladle the chicken zoodle soup into bowls. Garnish with chopped fresh parsley if desired. Serve hot with lemon wedges on the side for added brightness.

This chicken zoodle soup is not only delicious but also a lighter, low-carb option for those looking to reduce their carb intake. The zucchini noodles add a refreshing twist to the classic chicken soup. Feel free to customize the recipe by adding additional vegetables or herbs to suit your taste preferences.

Spinach and Artichoke Soup

Ingredients:

- 2 tablespoons butter
- 1 onion, finely chopped
- 3 cloves garlic, minced
- 1 can (14 oz) artichoke hearts, drained and chopped
- 4 cups fresh spinach, chopped
- 4 cups chicken or vegetable broth
- 1 cup heavy cream
- 1 cup shredded Parmesan cheese
- 8 oz cream cheese, softened
- Salt and black pepper, to taste
- Pinch of nutmeg (optional)
- Red pepper flakes, for garnish (optional)
- Chopped fresh parsley, for garnish

Instructions:

Sauté Vegetables:
- In a large pot, melt butter over medium heat. Add chopped onion and minced garlic. Sauté for 3-5 minutes until the onion is soft and translucent.

Add Artichokes and Spinach:
- Add the chopped artichoke hearts to the pot and cook for an additional 2-3 minutes. Stir in the chopped fresh spinach and cook until wilted.

Prepare Creamy Base:
- Reduce the heat to low and add cream cheese to the pot, stirring until it's melted and well combined with the vegetables.

Add Broth:
- Pour in the chicken or vegetable broth and bring the mixture to a simmer. Allow it to simmer for 10-15 minutes to let the flavors meld.

Blend Soup (Optional):
- For a smoother texture, use an immersion blender to blend the soup until creamy. If you prefer a chunkier texture, you can skip this step.

Add Heavy Cream and Parmesan:
- Stir in the heavy cream and shredded Parmesan cheese. Continue stirring until the cheese is melted and the soup is creamy.

Season:
- Season the soup with salt, black pepper, and a pinch of nutmeg (if using). Adjust the seasoning to taste.

Serve:
- Ladle the spinach and artichoke soup into bowls. Garnish with red pepper flakes and chopped fresh parsley. Serve hot and enjoy!

This soup is a delightful blend of creamy and savory, making it a comforting and satisfying dish. Serve it as a starter or enjoy it as a light meal with some crusty bread on the side. Feel free to customize the recipe to suit your taste preferences.

Salads:

Cobb Salad with Ranch Dressing

Ingredients:

For the Salad:

- 4 cups mixed salad greens (such as romaine lettuce, iceberg lettuce, or a spring mix)
- 2 cups cooked and diced chicken breast (grilled or roasted)
- 1 cup cherry tomatoes, halved
- 1 cup cooked bacon, crumbled
- 2 hard-boiled eggs, chopped
- 1 avocado, diced
- 1/2 cup crumbled blue cheese
- 1/4 cup sliced green onions (optional)
- Salt and black pepper, to taste

For the Ranch Dressing:

- 1/2 cup mayonnaise
- 1/2 cup sour cream
- 1 tablespoon chopped fresh chives
- 1 tablespoon chopped fresh parsley
- 1 teaspoon dried dill
- 1 teaspoon garlic powder
- 1 teaspoon onion powder
- Salt and black pepper, to taste
- 2-3 tablespoons buttermilk (optional, for thinning)

Instructions:

Prepare the Ranch Dressing:
- In a bowl, whisk together mayonnaise, sour cream, chives, parsley, dried dill, garlic powder, onion powder, salt, and black pepper. If you prefer a thinner dressing, you can add buttermilk a tablespoon at a time until you reach your desired consistency. Refrigerate until ready to use.

Assemble the Salad:

- Arrange the mixed salad greens on a large serving platter or individual plates.

Organize Ingredients:
- Organize the diced chicken, cherry tomatoes, crumbled bacon, chopped eggs, diced avocado, crumbled blue cheese, and sliced green onions (if using) into rows on top of the salad greens.

Season:
- Season the salad with salt and black pepper to taste.

Drizzle with Ranch Dressing:
- Drizzle the ranch dressing over the Cobb Salad. You can use as much or as little dressing as you prefer.

Serve:
- Serve the Cobb Salad immediately, offering additional ranch dressing on the side if desired.

This Cobb Salad with Ranch Dressing is a satisfying and well-balanced meal that showcases a variety of flavors and textures. It's perfect for a quick and delicious lunch or dinner, and you can easily customize it based on your preferences. Enjoy!

Greek Salad with Feta and Olives

Ingredients:

For the Salad:

- 4 cups chopped Romaine lettuce or mixed salad greens
- 1 cucumber, diced
- 1 cup cherry tomatoes, halved
- 1 red onion, thinly sliced
- 1 cup Kalamata olives, pitted
- 1 cup crumbled feta cheese
- 1/2 cup chopped fresh parsley

For the Dressing:

- 1/4 cup extra virgin olive oil
- 2 tablespoons red wine vinegar
- 1 teaspoon dried oregano
- Salt and black pepper, to taste

Instructions:

- Prepare the Salad:
    - In a large salad bowl, combine the chopped Romaine lettuce or mixed greens, diced cucumber, cherry tomatoes, sliced red onion, Kalamata olives, crumbled feta cheese, and chopped fresh parsley.
- Make the Dressing:
    - In a small bowl, whisk together the extra virgin olive oil, red wine vinegar, dried oregano, salt, and black pepper. Adjust the seasoning to taste.
- Drizzle the Dressing:
    - Drizzle the dressing over the salad. Toss the salad gently to coat the ingredients evenly with the dressing.
- Serve:
    - Serve the Greek Salad immediately, garnishing with additional feta cheese and olives if desired.

This Greek Salad is a colorful and nutritious option that's perfect as a side dish or a light meal. The combination of fresh vegetables, salty olives, and tangy feta cheese creates a delightful medley of flavors. Enjoy it on its own or as a complement to grilled meats or fish.

Avocado and Shrimp Salad

Ingredients:

For the Salad:

- 1 lb (450g) large shrimp, peeled and deveined
- 2 avocados, diced
- 1 cup cherry tomatoes, halved
- 1 cucumber, diced
- 1/4 cup red onion, finely chopped
- 1/4 cup fresh cilantro or parsley, chopped
- Mixed salad greens (optional)

For the Dressing:

- 2 tablespoons olive oil
- 2 tablespoons fresh lime juice
- 1 clove garlic, minced
- Salt and black pepper, to taste

Instructions:

Cook the Shrimp:
- In a large skillet, heat olive oil over medium-high heat. Add the shrimp and cook for 2-3 minutes per side until they turn pink and opaque. Season with salt and black pepper to taste. Remove from heat and set aside.

Prepare the Vegetables:
- In a large salad bowl, combine the diced avocados, cherry tomatoes, diced cucumber, chopped red onion, and fresh cilantro or parsley. If you prefer, you can also add mixed salad greens to the bowl.

Assemble the Salad:
- Add the cooked shrimp to the bowl with the vegetables.

Make the Dressing:
- In a small bowl, whisk together the olive oil, fresh lime juice, minced garlic, salt, and black pepper.

Drizzle with Dressing:

- Drizzle the dressing over the salad and shrimp. Gently toss to coat the ingredients evenly.

Serve:
- Serve the Avocado and Shrimp Salad immediately, either as a standalone dish or over a bed of mixed salad greens.

This salad is not only delicious but also a great source of healthy fats and protein. The combination of creamy avocado and succulent shrimp with the fresh vegetables creates a well-balanced and flavorful meal. Enjoy it for a quick lunch, a light dinner, or as a refreshing appetizer.

Kale and Walnut Salad with Lemon Vinaigrette

Ingredients:

For the Salad:

- 1 bunch kale, stems removed and leaves thinly sliced
- 1 cup cherry tomatoes, halved
- 1/2 cup crumbled feta cheese
- 1/2 cup chopped walnuts, toasted
- 1/4 cup red onion, thinly sliced

For the Lemon Vinaigrette:

- 1/4 cup extra virgin olive oil
- 2 tablespoons fresh lemon juice
- 1 teaspoon Dijon mustard
- 1 clove garlic, minced
- Salt and black pepper, to taste

Instructions:

Prepare the Kale:
- In a large salad bowl, add the thinly sliced kale. Massage the kale leaves with your hands for a few minutes to soften them and enhance the flavor.

Add Toppings:
- Add the cherry tomatoes, crumbled feta cheese, toasted walnuts, and thinly sliced red onion to the bowl with the kale.

Make the Lemon Vinaigrette:
- In a small bowl, whisk together the extra virgin olive oil, fresh lemon juice, Dijon mustard, minced garlic, salt, and black pepper.

Drizzle with Dressing:
- Drizzle the lemon vinaigrette over the salad. Toss the salad gently to ensure all ingredients are coated with the dressing.

Let it Marinate:
- Allow the salad to marinate for a few minutes before serving. This helps the kale absorb the flavors and become more tender.

Serve:
- Serve the Kale and Walnut Salad with Lemon Vinaigrette as a refreshing and nutritious side dish or add grilled chicken or another protein for a complete meal.

This salad is not only delicious but also packed with nutrients. The combination of kale, walnuts, and lemon vinaigrette creates a delightful balance of flavors and textures. Enjoy this salad as a healthy addition to your meals!

Tuna Salad Lettuce Wraps

Ingredients:

For the Tuna Salad:

- 2 cans (5 oz each) canned tuna, drained
- 1/4 cup mayonnaise
- 1 tablespoon Dijon mustard
- 2 celery stalks, finely chopped
- 1/4 red onion, finely chopped
- 1 tablespoon fresh lemon juice
- Salt and black pepper, to taste
- Optional: 1-2 tablespoons chopped fresh parsley or dill

For the Lettuce Wraps:

- Large lettuce leaves (such as iceberg or Romaine)
- Avocado slices (optional)
- Tomato slices (optional)
- Cucumber slices (optional)

Instructions:

Prepare the Tuna Salad:
- In a bowl, combine the drained tuna, mayonnaise, Dijon mustard, chopped celery, chopped red onion, fresh lemon juice, salt, and black pepper. Mix well until all ingredients are thoroughly combined. Add chopped fresh parsley or dill if desired for added flavor.

Assemble the Lettuce Wraps:
- Lay out large lettuce leaves on a clean surface. Spoon a portion of the tuna salad onto the center of each lettuce leaf.

Add Optional Ingredients:
- If desired, add slices of avocado, tomato, and cucumber on top of the tuna salad.

Wrap and Serve:

- Gently fold the sides of the lettuce leaves over the tuna salad and optional ingredients, creating a wrap. Secure with toothpicks if needed.

Serve:
- Arrange the Tuna Salad Lettuce Wraps on a platter and serve immediately.

These Tuna Salad Lettuce Wraps are not only quick to prepare but also a healthy and satisfying choice for a light meal or snack. They are customizable, and you can add your favorite vegetables or herbs to enhance the flavor. Enjoy this low-carb alternative to traditional sandwiches!

Dips:

Baba Ganoush

Ingredients:

- 2 medium-sized eggplants
- 1/4 cup tahini (sesame paste)
- 2 cloves garlic, minced
- 2 tablespoons fresh lemon juice
- 2 tablespoons extra virgin olive oil, plus more for drizzling
- Salt, to taste
- 1 tablespoon chopped fresh parsley (for garnish, optional)
- Pomegranate seeds (for garnish, optional)

Instructions:

Roast the Eggplants:
- Preheat the oven to 400°F (200°C). Prick the eggplants with a fork in a few places. Place them on a baking sheet and roast in the oven for about 40-45 minutes or until the skin is charred, and the flesh is soft.

Cool and Peel:
- Allow the roasted eggplants to cool. Once cooled, peel off the charred skin, leaving the soft flesh.

Prepare the Baba Ganoush:
- In a food processor, combine the roasted eggplant flesh, tahini, minced garlic, fresh lemon juice, and extra virgin olive oil. Blend until smooth.

Season:
- Season the baba ganoush with salt to taste. Adjust the lemon juice, garlic, or tahini if needed, based on your preferences.

Serve:
- Transfer the baba ganoush to a serving bowl. Drizzle with additional olive oil and garnish with chopped fresh parsley and pomegranate seeds if desired.

Chill (Optional):
- For enhanced flavors, you can refrigerate the baba ganoush for a couple of hours before serving.

Serve:

- Serve the baba ganoush with pita bread, crackers, or fresh vegetables. Enjoy!

Baba Ganoush is a versatile dip that can be served as an appetizer, snack, or part of a mezze platter. It's a great way to enjoy the rich, smoky flavor of roasted eggplants. Feel free to adjust the ingredients to suit your taste preferences.

Spinach and Artichoke Dip

Ingredients:

- 1 (10-ounce) package frozen chopped spinach, thawed and drained
- 1 (14-ounce) can artichoke hearts, drained and chopped
- 1/2 cup mayonnaise
- 1/2 cup sour cream
- 1 cup grated Parmesan cheese
- 1 cup shredded mozzarella cheese
- 1 teaspoon minced garlic
- 1/4 teaspoon salt
- 1/4 teaspoon black pepper
- 1/4 teaspoon crushed red pepper flakes (optional, for a hint of heat)
- 1 tablespoon olive oil (for greasing the baking dish)
- Tortilla chips, pita bread, or sliced baguette for serving

Instructions:

Preheat the Oven:
- Preheat your oven to 375°F (190°C).

Prepare Spinach and Artichokes:
- Ensure the frozen spinach is thawed and well-drained. Chop the drained artichoke hearts into small pieces.

Mix Ingredients:
- In a large mixing bowl, combine the chopped spinach, chopped artichoke hearts, mayonnaise, sour cream, grated Parmesan cheese, shredded mozzarella cheese, minced garlic, salt, black pepper, and optional crushed red pepper flakes. Mix well until all ingredients are evenly combined.

Grease Baking Dish:
- Lightly grease a baking dish with olive oil. This can be a small casserole dish or a similar oven-safe container.

Bake:
- Transfer the mixture to the greased baking dish, spreading it out evenly. Bake in the preheated oven for about 25-30 minutes or until the dip is hot and bubbly, and the top is golden brown.

Serve:

- Remove from the oven and let it cool for a few minutes before serving. Serve the spinach and artichoke dip with tortilla chips, pita bread, or sliced baguette.

This Spinach and Artichoke Dip is perfect for parties, game nights, or any gathering. The creamy and cheesy texture combined with the savory spinach and artichoke flavors make it a favorite appetizer. Enjoy dipping!

Cilantro Lime Avocado Dip

Ingredients:

- 2 ripe avocados, peeled and pitted
- 1/4 cup fresh cilantro, chopped
- 1 clove garlic, minced
- Juice of 2 limes
- 1/2 teaspoon ground cumin
- Salt and black pepper, to taste
- Optional: 1 jalapeño, seeded and finely chopped (for a spicy kick)
- Optional: 1/4 cup red onion, finely chopped

Instructions:

Prepare Avocados:
- In a bowl, mash the ripe avocados with a fork until smooth.

Add Ingredients:
- Add chopped cilantro, minced garlic, lime juice, ground cumin, salt, and black pepper to the mashed avocados.

Optional Additions:
- If desired, add finely chopped jalapeño for some heat or red onion for added flavor.

Mix Well:
- Mix all the ingredients together until well combined.

Adjust Seasoning:
- Taste the dip and adjust the seasoning, adding more salt, pepper, or lime juice as needed.

Chill (Optional):
- For enhanced flavors, you can refrigerate the dip for about 30 minutes before serving.

Serve:
- Serve the Cilantro Lime Avocado Dip with tortilla chips, vegetable sticks, or as a topping for tacos and grilled meats.

This dip is not only delicious but also versatile. It can be used as a topping, a side dish, or a flavorful spread. The combination of creamy avocado, zesty lime, and fresh cilantro creates a bright and tasty dip that's perfect for various occasions. Enjoy!

Pimento Cheese Dip

Ingredients:

- 2 cups sharp cheddar cheese, shredded
- 1/2 cup mayonnaise
- 4 oz cream cheese, softened
- 1/2 cup diced pimentos, drained
- 1/4 teaspoon garlic powder
- 1/4 teaspoon onion powder
- 1/4 teaspoon cayenne pepper (optional, for a hint of heat)
- Salt and black pepper, to taste
- Crackers, bread, or vegetable sticks for serving

Instructions:

Prepare the Ingredients:
- Ensure that the cream cheese is softened. Drain the diced pimentos if they are packed in liquid.

Mix Cheeses:
- In a mixing bowl, combine the shredded sharp cheddar cheese, softened cream cheese, and mayonnaise.

Add Pimentos and Seasoning:
- Add the diced pimentos, garlic powder, onion powder, cayenne pepper (if using), salt, and black pepper to the cheese mixture.

Combine Well:
- Mix all the ingredients together until well combined. You can use a spoon or an electric mixer for a smoother consistency.

Adjust Seasoning:
- Taste the pimento cheese dip and adjust the seasoning, adding more salt or pepper if needed.

Chill (Optional):
- For enhanced flavors, you can refrigerate the dip for at least 30 minutes before serving.

Serve:
- Serve the Pimento Cheese Dip with crackers, sliced baguette, or vegetable sticks.

This Pimento Cheese Dip is a versatile and crowd-pleasing appetizer. It's perfect for parties, picnics, or as a tasty spread for sandwiches. Feel free to customize the recipe by adding your favorite herbs or spices. Enjoy!

Roasted Red Pepper Hummus

Ingredients:

- 1 can (15 oz) chickpeas (garbanzo beans), drained and rinsed
- 1/3 cup tahini (sesame paste)
- 1/4 cup extra virgin olive oil, plus more for drizzling
- 1/4 cup fresh lemon juice (about 1 large lemon)
- 2 cloves garlic, minced
- 1/2 teaspoon ground cumin
- 1/2 teaspoon smoked paprika
- 1/2 cup roasted red peppers (store-bought or homemade), drained
- Salt and black pepper, to taste
- Optional: Crushed red pepper flakes for a hint of heat
- Optional: Chopped fresh parsley or cilantro for garnish

Instructions:

Prepare Chickpeas:
- Drain and rinse the chickpeas under cold water.

Combine Ingredients:
- In a food processor, combine chickpeas, tahini, olive oil, fresh lemon juice, minced garlic, ground cumin, smoked paprika, and roasted red peppers.

Blend:
- Blend the ingredients until smooth and creamy. You may need to stop and scrape down the sides of the food processor to ensure everything is well mixed.

Season:
- Season the hummus with salt and black pepper to taste. Add optional crushed red pepper flakes for a bit of heat.

Adjust Consistency:
- If the hummus is too thick, you can add a bit more olive oil or water, one tablespoon at a time, until you reach your desired consistency.

Serve:
- Transfer the Roasted Red Pepper Hummus to a serving bowl. Drizzle with extra virgin olive oil and garnish with chopped fresh parsley or cilantro if desired.

Chill (Optional):

- For enhanced flavors, refrigerate the hummus for at least 30 minutes before serving.

Serve:
- Serve the Roasted Red Pepper Hummus with pita bread, crackers, vegetable sticks, or as a spread for sandwiches and wraps.

This Roasted Red Pepper Hummus is a flavorful and colorful dip that's perfect for snacking or entertaining. Enjoy the sweet and smoky notes from the roasted red peppers in this delicious variation of classic hummus!

www.ingramcontent.com/pod-product-compliance
Lightning Source LLC
LaVergne TN
LVHW081605060526
838201LV00054B/2087